Understanding Fasting

Mark H. Ballard

Bennington, Vermont

Understanding Fasting
Copyright © 2025 by Mark H. Ballard

Published by Northeastern Baptist Press
Post Office Box 4600
Bennington, VT 05201

Scripture taken from the New King James Version®.
Copyright © 1982 by Thomas Nelson. Used by permission.
All rights reserved.

Softcover ISBN: 978-1-953331-61-8

To Cindy and Ben

PREFACE

In the Fall of 2002 Pastor Ballard sensed the Lord leading him to call Christian Fellowship to 40 days of intense focus on the Lord. As he continued to seek the Lord as to the nature of the 40 Days several elements developed into a cohesive unit which he called "40 Days of Focus." Early in the development process Pastor Ballard sensed that the spiritual exercise of fasting needed to play a major role in the time of focus. Knowing fasting to be a subject of much misunderstanding, he set out to provide a brief introduction for the congregation.

The material in this booklet was originally presented to the congregation on the first Sunday of the "40 Days of Focus" during the Sunday School / Bible Study hour. Realizing that fasting is a little practiced and much misunderstood spiritual exercise; it was decided to turn the material into a booklet that could be distributed.

Our prayer is that the Lord will use this material in your life to draw you closer to Him. May the Lord bless you as you read *Understanding Fasting*.

INTRODUCTION

Fasting is a spiritual activity not often discussed, and practiced even less. However, even a cursory scan of the Scriptures clearly reveals that fasting should be a part of the life of every believer. I am convinced that one of the reasons fasting is not practiced much today is because much confusion surrounds the topic. Though this brief booklet cannot cover every aspect relating to fasting I trust that it will provide a basic introduction that will help you in your spiritual growth. In this booklet we will consider seven basic questions relating to fasting. Having posed the question, we will attempt to gain a basic understanding of the topic posed. The seven questions we will attempt to answer are: What is fasting? What is the Purpose of Fasting? What are the Various Types of Fasts? How Long Should I Fast? What about my Health? What should I do when I Fast? and, Can Fasting Be Misused?

Having considered the issues posed by each of the seven questions the reader should have a good working knowledge of the basics of the spiritual exercise of fasting. As you read the information found in the coming pages ask the Lord to open your eyes to understand His purpose for fasting in your own life.

WHAT IS FASTING?

Most Christians today have heard of fasting but are not certain what it is all about. In order to gain an understanding of the concept of fasting let's begin with the word itself. The Bible speaks of fasting in both the Old and New Testaments. The Hebrew word *tsuwm* or *tsoom* is translated as fast in the Old Testament. The word simply means to abstain from food. Likewise, the Greek word *nesteuo*, translated as fast in the New Testament, means to abstain as a religious exercise, from food and drink. These two words give a basic understanding of what fasting is all about.

Essentially there are two key elements we should learn from these words. First, we should note, in the Bible, fasting has to do with the abstention from eating and sometimes even from drinking. Over the years some Christian leaders have included other types of fasts, which we will mention later in this booklet. However, in the Scriptures the concept of fasting always has to do with the avoidance of food and drink.

The second thing we should note comes from the Greek Word *nesteuo*. As previously noted, *nesteuo* conveys the idea that the abstention from food has a religious purpose. Biblical fasting is going without food and possibly drink for a spiritual cause. There are many reasons that people go without food. People go without food

2

because of financial distress, medical tests, depression, illnesses, or even as part of a weight loss diet. However, none of these reasons qualify as a Biblical Fast. For a fast to be Biblically based one must go without food for a spiritual purpose.

Having identified the fact that one must fast with a spiritual purpose for their fast to be Biblical, we must now turn our attention to understanding what qualifies as a spiritual purpose for going without food. This is the focus of our next question.

WHAT IS THE PURPOSE OF FASTING?

God made us in such a way that we need and we are to enjoy food. From the beginning of creation God made everything necessary for mankind to live. As we consume food it fuels our bodies to perform as they should. In addition, we find the consumption of food as part of celebrations throughout history. Most of the celebrations described in Scripture included feasting and special meals of celebration. Yet the Scriptures clearly reveal that there are times and specific reasons that the normal consumption of food should be set aside to accomplish a spiritual purpose.

Tony Evans in his book entitled, *Tony Evans Speaks Out On Fasting*[1] identifies several general reasons for fasting, as well as, a few specific times one should focus on fasting. Tony basis his discussion of the purpose of fasting on Isaiah 58:4. "Indeed you fast for strife and debate, And to strike with the fist of wickedness. You will not fast as you do this day, To make your voice heard on high." He focuses attention on the last phrase of the verse: "...To make your voice heard on high." He points out that fasting gives us an opportunity to humble ourselves before God, sharpen our spiritual focus, and adjust our priorities to the spiritual rather than the physical or material.

In the balance of his book, Evans discusses three specific reasons one should fast. He speaks of fasting for the purpose of healing, for protection, and fasting for ministry. With each purpose he presents Biblical Examples including Hannah (I Samuel 1), Esther (Esther 4:16), and the Church at Antioch (Acts 13:1-3).

Elmer Towns' book titled, *Fasting For Spiritual Break Through* is based entirely on Isaiah 58:6-8.[2]

Is this not the fast that I have chosen: To loose the bonds of wickedness, To undo the heavy

---

1   Evans, Tony. *Tony Evans Speaks Out On Fasting.* Chicago: Moody Press, 2000.

2   Towns, Elmer. *Fasting for Spiritual Breakthrough.* Minneapolis: Bethany House, 2017.

burdens, To let the oppressed go free, And that you break every yoke? Is it not to share your bread with the hungry, And that you bring to your house the poor who are cast out; When you see the naked, that you cover him, And not hide yourself from your own flesh? Then your light shall break forth like the morning, Your healing shall spring forth speedily, And your righteousness shall go before you; The glory of the LORD shall be your rear guard.

Townes' entire book demonstrates the fact that these verses identify nine specific reasons to fast. For each purpose Towns identifies a Biblical Character to whom we can look to as an example. Below you will find a list of the Biblical Character and the purpose of his/her fast, along with the Scripture reference where you can learn about their fast.

The Disciples Fast
-    Matthew 17:14-21
-    Purpose: Freedom from addiction

The Ezra Fast
-    Ezra 8:21-23
-    Purpose: To solve a problem

The Samuel Fast
- Samuel 7:1-8
- Purpose: For evangelism & revival

The Elijah Fast
- 1Kings 19:2-18
- Purpose: To deal with fear

The Widow's Fast
- 1Kings 17:12
- Purpose: To provide for the needy

The Saint Paul Fast
- Acts 9:9-19
- Purpose: For insight into decisions we must make

The Daniel Fast
- Daniel 1:12-20
- Purpose: For physical health & healing

The John The Baptist Fast
- Matthew 3:4 & Luke 1:15
- Purpose: For an influential testimony

The Esther Fast
- Esther 4:16
- Purpose: For protection

Neither Evans nor Towns give a complete list of reasons one can or should fast. However, between the two books we begin to gain an understanding of the purpose of fasting. If one is to fast Biblically, there must be a spiritual purpose behind the abstention from food.

Essentially, the purpose of fasting is to **FOCUS OUR FAITH ON THE FATHER'S FACE**. The idea here is that we need Him so desperately that we are willing to forego the normal consumption of food to focus our attention beyond the things of this life. Rather, we focus completely on Him. We are seeking His Face. We need Him to act. We need Him to do something that only He can do. Our situation is beyond our control, and we humbly seek our Gracious Lord's intervention. We may need Him to act in our own life, in the life of our family, our church, our nation, or the life of a friend. By fasting we are setting aside the normal necessities of food and humbly acknowledging our desperate need of God to work in our situation.

WHAT ARE THE VARIOUS TYPES OF FASTS?

Over the last fifty years or so there have been Christian leaders who have identified various types of fasts, including fasts that have nothing to do with the abstention from food. Although it may be spiritually beneficial to abstain from television, radio, entertainment, and the like; these so-called fasts do not find their basis in Scripture. As noted earlier the words used in both the Old and New Testaments speak to the issue of food and drink. Therefore, a Biblical fast is about abstention from normal physical nourishment. There are three basic types of fasts as observed in Scripture. Let's take a brief look at all three.

The Total Fast

The Total fast is where a person abstains from **ALL** forms of food and drink. In Exodus 34:28 we learn of Moses fasting before the Lord for forty days. His fast was a total fast where he neither "ate bread nor drank water." Moses' experience was no doubt a miraculous event. Though there have been many people that have gone such a long time without food, to go so long without water required divine intervention. One must be certain of the Lord's leading to go without liquids. This is rare even in Scripture discussions of fasting.

The Partial Fast

Daniel and his three Hebrew friends stand as excellent examples of a partial fast. In Daniel chapter 1 we learn that they were being held captive in Babylon. The plan was to prepare these four Hebrew captives to serve as special servants to the king. Part of their preparation included the eating of food that was against the commandment of the Lord for these young men to consume. At the leading of the Lord, Daniel requested that they be allowed to participate in a partial fast. The young men would eat vegetables, but they would abstain from all forms of meat for a period of time. Now we know there were certain meats a Jewish young man was not to eat, however, there were also some meats that they could eat; and during feast times were even required to eat. Yet on this occasion Daniel requested he and his friends be allowed this partial fast. The Lord clearly honored their fast and blessed them greatly for their faithfulness.

There may be times that the Lord will lead you to a partial fast. On these occasions you may lay aside certain foods and/or drinks that are part of your normal diet. You are setting these aside for a particular spiritual reason and for a specified period of time. During this time, you should seek the Lord's Face for a specific issue in your life.

The Typical Fast

Towns refers to this type as the "Normal Fast."[3] The typical fast that is most often observed in Scripture relates to

---

3   Towns. *Fasting...Breakthrough.* 22.

the avoidance of all food items during a specified period of time for a spiritual purpose. Luke 4:1-2 describes for us Jesus' Forty-day fast as a time where "He ate nothing." This is the pattern most often found in the Bible. Solid foods are avoided but liquids are received.

Some would argue that only water should be received during the fast. Others would encourage juices and possibly even broth during fasts that extend for several days. Typically, when I fast, I avoid all food and accept only water, coffee, and sometimes fruit juices. It is not necessary to become legalistic in your interpretation of the definition of liquids. This can be left up to the individual to determine as the Lord leads their time of fasting.

How Long Should I Fast?

The question of the length of the fast has been debated by many leaders who practice fasting. There are two basic positions on the issue. One position holds that the length of the fast should be left open. This view argues that one should fast until God responds or leads them to break the fast. The emphasis here is placed on relying on the Holy Spirit to lead you as to when it is time to stop the fast.

The second view takes the position that the length of the fast should be pre-set so that one does not simply quit when it gets difficult. This position would point out times in Scripture where the duration of the fast was pre-determined. Examples of this can be seen in Leviticus 23:27 and in 1 Samuel 14:24.

Though I believe both positions have merit I tend to follow the later idea of a pre-set time for the fast. Using this method I would still want to be sensitive to the leading of the Holy Spirit in my life. Therefore, I would seek His leading as to the length prior to starting. Once the fast has begun I should make every effort to complete the allotted time. Of course, the Spirit has the prerogative to add to a fast or end one early, and when the Spirit leads, we have the responsibility to be sensitive and obedient to His leading.

On one occasion in my life, it became clear that the Spirit was leading me to shorten my fast. I struggled with it for a few days, but as I sought the Lord, it became clear that indeed, He was leading me to complete the fast earlier than I had planned. Knowing the Lord's leading, I ended the fast early, had a strong sense of the Lord's peace in my life, and was confident that I had acted at the Lord's leading.

In the appendix to his book *Fasting For Spiritual Break Through*[4], Towns points out several Biblical examples of the duration of various fasts. These examples include: partial-day, one-day, three-day, seven-day, fourteen-day, three-week and forty-day fasts. Let me simply mention

---

4   Towns. *Fasting...breakthrough*, 205ff.

here that one should be careful in participating in an extended fast. Most people's health can handle a partial-day, one-day or three-day fast without major complications. However, it is recommended that one consult with their physician before beginning an extended fast. In fact, there are several health issues that must be considered when one decides to fast.

WHAT ABOUT MY HEALTH?

There is no doubt that God is more concerned with your health than anyone else. The fact is God has a lot more to say about our health than most of us are willing to admit. Though at times the Lord uses illness to get our attention or to show forth His power, for the most part the Lord wants us to be in the best health possible in order that we can serve Him to the fullest. Yet, He is most concerned with our spiritual health. Therefore, at times it is prudent to forego the normal patterns of eating to focus on spiritual health.

Though the primary purpose of fasting is spiritual the process can also benefit us physically. In his book *What the Bible Says About Healthy Living*[5], Rex Russell, M.D. discusses the issue of fasting as it relates to physi-

---

5 Russell, Rex. *What the Bible Says about Healthy Living.* Grand Rapids: Revell, 2006.

cal health. Russell points out that there are at least four physical benefits received from fasting.

Having stated that fasting has physical benefits does not ignore the fact that there are health issues that can be a hindrance to fasting. For instance, a person with hypoglycemia (low blood sugar) or hyperglycemia (high blood sugar) could be negatively impacted by fasting. In fact, fasting could be very dangerous to persons with these and other medical illnesses. Therefore, it is always wise to consult your physician before entering a fast.

In consulting your physician, you may find it is absolutely impossible for you to participate in a total fast or possibly even a typical fast. In these cases, let me suggest that you consider the partial fast. Seek your doctor's advice in determining what parts of your normal diet that you could avoid during your special time of focus.

Almost everyone I have ever met had certain things that were a part of their diet that they could avoid for a pre-set period of time. Remember that fasting is not simply the avoidance of food. The avoidance must be accompanied by a time of seeking God's Face for a spiritual purpose.

One further word concerning your health must be discussed. It is crucial that when you determine the length of your fast you should consider your health. Even if you believe yourself to be in good health, extended periods of fasting should be undertaken only after consulting your physician. Remember the Bible represents at least 5000 years of human history, and only three times does it speak of the forty-day fast. Many Biblical Leaders fasted, but we are only told of three who fasted forty days: Moses, Elijah, and Jesus.

The Lord may someday lead you to fast beyond one meal. He may lead you to fast one day or even one week. It is possible that He may even call you to a forty-day fast. If you are considering a forty day fast let me suggest the following:

1. Make certain it is the Lord's leading
2. Consult your physician
3. Read the experience of others who have done it (see book list at the end of this booklet for Ronnie Floyd & Bill Bright)
4. Speak with someone who has done it
5. Follow your doctor's advice on preparing for and ending the fast

What should I do when I Fast?

In discussing this question, we will consider three primary issues relating to fasting. First, we will look at what to do to prepare for a fast. Next, we will turn our attention to what to do during the fast itself. Finally, we will focus on what to do as you end the fast.

The Preparation For The Fast

When you have determined that the Lord is calling you to fast you should prepare yourself. Many times, you will be able to prepare yourself over a period of several days. Sometimes however, the Lord may lead you to begin a fast rather quickly. Either way there are certain things you should do to prepare yourself. First, you should prepare yourself spiritually. Then you should prepare yourself physically.

Spiritually, you should spend time praying about the fast prior to beginning the process. Let me suggest several ways to prepare yourself spiritually.

1. Clarify your spiritual purpose for fasting
2. Ask the Lord to empower you to complete the fast
3. Ask the Lord to make you sensitive to Him
4. Ask the Lord to reveal any sin that needs addressed
5. Read passages of Scripture that relate to fasting

You also need to prepare yourself physically for the fast. Some folks who are new to fasting think that they should eat a large meal prior to fasting to kind of "hold them over" so to speak. This usually has the opposite effect on your body. Exactly how you prepare yourself physically will be determined by the length of your fast. Once again here is a good place to consult your physician.

Personally, I make very little physical preparation if the fast is for one day. However, the longer the fast, the more important it is to prepare your body for the physical changes it is about to experience.

The Participation of The Fast

Concerning the fast itself, in his booklet *7 Basic Steps To Successful Fasting & Prayer*[6], Bill Bright suggests you put yourself on a schedule when you fast. Plan to use the time you would normally be eating to focus on the Father. Spend that time with Him in prayer, Bible reading, and meditating on Scripture. Spend time worshiping the Lord, seeking His presence, power and purpose for your life. Seek the Lord's face concerning the purpose of your fast. Talk to Him about the reason you are fasting at every opportunity. Set aside time to "Be still..." before Him and to simply "Wait on the Lord..."

Whenever the Lord reveals something to you write it down, then act on it. For instance, He may show you sin in your life that you need to address. Confess it, forsake it, and experience His forgiveness. He may impress

---

6   Bright, Bill. *7 Basic Steps To Successful Fasting & Prayer.* New Life Publications, 1995.

a Scriptural truth upon your life. Write it down, meditate on it, obey it. He may impress you to do something for Him, to talk to someone about Him, or to talk to Him about someone. Be sensitive to His promptings in your life and obey His leading.

Many have found it helpful to keep a journal during times of fasting. This process can help you clarify what God is doing in your life through the fast. It can also be a great help in the future as you reflect back on what God teaches you during this time of spiritual focus. It may even enable you to encourage others with your experience of fasting.

The most important thing here is to stay focused as you fast. Going without food alone will not accomplish much. You must be focused on the purpose of your fast. If you are fasting for revival in your church, let that be the focus. If you are fasting for a Spiritual Awakening in your country, let this be your focus. If you are fasting to seek God's direction in your life, let that be your focus. You may have 2 or 3 reasons for which you are fasting. Whatever the purpose, stay focused on seeking the Lord's Face concerning that purpose throughout the entirety of your fast.

The Consummation of The Fast

As you bring your fast to a conclusion, you should do so in a spirit of praise and celebration. You may or may not have received the answer you were looking for during your time of fasting, but if you have sought the Lord and spent time with Him you will have surely grown through the process. You will have a new sense of intimacy with the Father. You will have a better perspective on your walk with Him, and He will have taught you some things along the way. Therefore, end the time with rejoicing and praise. Your first meal should be planned and should be celebratory in nature.

The length of your fast should help you determine what you eat for your first meal. For instance, if you fasted one meal, what you eat is not as important as if you fasted for a week or more. If you fast for a day, it may be helpful to have a light meal as you break your fast. This is especially true if you fast for 2 or 3 days. If you fast for a week or longer you may want to begin with broth, soups, fruit, etc; then slowly add in the items from your regular diet. Once again, this is a good thing to discuss with your doctor before you begin your fast.

As you conclude your fast remember what God taught you during the process. Conclude not only in praise and celebration but with a commitment to be obedient to the Father. Take all that you learned and tuck it away in your heart.

Can Fasting Be Misused?

There is no doubt that fasting can be abused and misused. One of the clearest examples of the misuse of fasting is found in the life of the Pharisees in Jesus' day. Fasting had become nothing more than a religious ritual to perform. They fasted physically but their hearts were far from God.

In the appendix to his book *Fasting For Spiritual Break Through*[7], Elmer Towns reveals at least five misuses of fasting found in Scripture including: 1. The separation of the physical act from the spiritual devotion, 2. Fasting to attempt to cover sinful motives and actions, 3. Fasting for economic reasons, 4. Fasting to look spiritual in the eyes of other people, and 5. Demanding others to fast.

Let me suggest a few things to help you avoid the misuse of fasting.

1. Have a spiritual purpose for fasting.
2. Do not fast just to look spiritual to others.
3. Focus on seeking the Father's Face as you fast.
4. Focus on the purpose of your fast.
5. Focus on humbling yourself before the Lord.
6. Focus on drawing closer to Him through the process.
7. Never demand others join you in your fast.

---

7 Towns. *Fasting...breakthrough*, 205ff.

CONCLUSION

Although fasting is no where commanded in the New Testament, the Bible clearly demonstrates that God has a special blessing for those who fast with the proper motivation. Fasting can impact your life, your family, your church, your country, and your world. I trust the principles discussed in this booklet will help you in your journey to walk with the Lord. I pray you will ask the Lord if He would have you to join Him in the journey of fasting. If He calls you to a fast remember to clarify your purpose, prepare for the fast, stay focused during the fast, and break the fast with an attitude of praise and celebration.

I believe that in these later days God is calling many of His people to prayer and fasting for our nation. Could it be that He is calling you to fast and pray for one more Spiritual Awakening in this Land? Will you answer His call?

Resources on Fasting

Bill Bright
- *7 Basic Steps To Successful Fasting & Prayer*
- *The Transforming Power Of Fasting & Prayer: Personal Accounts of Spiritual Renewal*

Tony Evans
- *Tony Evans Speaks Out On Fasting*

Ronnie Floyd
- *The Power of Prayer & Fasting*

Elmer Towns
- *The Beginner's Guide to Fasting*
- *Knowing God Through Fasting Fasting For Spiritual Break Through*

Arthur Wallis
- *God's Chosen Fast*